AMERICAN
WISDOM

ALBERT BENDER

PREMIUM
PRESS
AMERICA

Native American Wisdom
©2015 Albert Bender

ISBN 978-1-887654-97-5

Library of Congress Catalog Card Number: 2014959153
Published by Premium Press America

Premium Press America books are available at special discounts for
premiums, sales promotions, fundraising, or educational use. For details
contact the distributor at 6581 Jocelyn Hollow Road, Nashville TN 37205-
3950, phone toll-free 800-891-7323, fax 615-353-7905, or email orders@
premiumpressamerica.com

www.premiumpressamerica.com

Printed in the United States of America
10 9 8 7 6 5 4 3 2 1

To the memory of Cherokee elder
Marian Dunn,
a powerful advocate of Native culture
and traditions and an inspiration to
all who knew her. As a historian and
storyteller she passed on her knowledge
to those blessed to listen.

Introduction

This small volume is meant to acquaint readers with an abundance of facts concerning Native Americans—both ancient and contemporary—that are not known to the general public. Many of these facts are important, amazing, and at the very least, all are of great interest.

In pre-contact times the people of the Americas were physical and social scientists, advanced agriculturists, (two-thirds of the world's crops have Native American origins), physicians (U.S. pharmaceutical industry is based on Indian medicines), general surgeons (Indigenous doctors in North America, Central and South America were performing complex and delicate operations hundreds of years ago), merchants (vast trade networks existed throughout the Americas), plastic surgeons, mathematicians (Ancient Olmecs developed the concept of zero), architects, urban planners (large Native cities existed from the U.S. Midwest, Southeast and Southwest to Central and South America), poets, engineers, astronomers, anesthesiologists, cartographers, artists, metallurgists, optical technologists, road builders, brain surgeons, psychologists, carpenters, musicians, stone masons, plumbers, dentists, scribes, ecologists, orators, environmentalists, botanists, musicians, and political scientists.

Native Americans were all of the above and more, and are to this very day. The author, who is Cherokee Indian, pulls many entries from his own personal knowledge. This writer, also been a tribal attorney for various tribes and also a chief tribal court judge. Moreover, The author's family who went west by the Treaty of Cherokee Agency of 1817 passed down many stories of the travails, tragedies and conflicts of those times. Further, the author is a reporter on contemporary Native issues, for various newspapers Native and non-Native, many of which are fraught with tragedy. But, at the request of the publisher, to which there was hearty agreement, the information contained in this volume has to do with great achievements and interesting facts. Readers will relish in finding facts they never heard about American Indians—many that will surprise and astound.

–Albert Bender

Native American, American Indian, Native American Indian, Original Peoples, First Nations: These are all terms for the native people of the Americas. Most Natives in the United States now seem to prefer the term *American Indian*.

The state with the largest Native American population is Oklahoma. More than thirty-nine tribes reside in the state.

The name *Manhattan*, now known as a borough of New York City, is from an ancient Indian tribe affiliated with the Lenni-Lenape (Delaware) Nation. The name means "Hilly Island."

The term *papoose*, which has come to mean a Native infant, is from the Narragansett Indian word *papu* meaning "father." The term is now pretty much universally used.

The first American Indian physician, Dr. Carlos Montezuma, a Yavapai Indian from Arizona, graduated from Chicago Medical College in 1889. He was taken captive and raised by a minister who lived in Illinois.

Wampum is a word in the Narragansett language for shell beads. It is thought that the first wampum beads were made by that Rhode Island tribe. Later, the practice spread and other tribal nations, including the Iroquois in New York and the Cherokee in the South, made wampum belts to memorialize such important events as treaties and friendship between tribes and colonists.

Most Native American populations in large cities were relocated to urban areas in the 1950s by the Bureau of Indian Affairs to try to assimilate them into mainstream society.

There are 310 American Indian reservations in the U.S. and 566 federally recognized Indian nations in the country—which means that not all tribal nations have reservations. Some tribes share reservations; some peoples have more than one reservation. For example, the Sioux have about fourteen reservations. The Apaches have around seven. More than one thousand tribes are now waiting for recognition.

Pow wows are gatherings of Native Americans for a celebratory, social, religious, and friendship event to which the general public is invited. The pow wows replicate the ancient Indian trade fairs of thousands of years ago. In olden times, different peoples gathered regionally to exchange their arts, crafts, food, and clothing apparel.

Writing systems existed among Native peoples in North and Central America. The Ojibwa used a system of symbols carved on birch bark scrolls to record songs, healing rituals, herbal knowledge, and genealogical records. The Iroquois used wampum beads woven into sashes to record important events.

In the 1830s at a dinner meeting between Cherokees and federal officials in Washington, D.C., one white man mockingly said, "Cherokees just live on roots." A Cherokee leader, seeing a plate of sweet potatoes, said, "Pass me the roots." The joke was on the white guy, and everyone had a good laugh.

Many Native American tribes kept records by pictures or symbols. Pictographs were drawn on bark or hide, or etched in stone.

The piñon is a variety of pine tree that produces edible nuts. The author has been at Native gatherings in the Southwest and heard someone say of piñon nuts, "Betcha you can't eat just one." Just as in potato chips, they were right.

When first observing white people reading from a book, the Cherokees called the writing "Talking Leaves." On the Eastern Cherokee Reservation in North Carolina, one of the largest bookstores with a huge collection of Indian literature is named Talking Leaves.

Native Nations throughout the United States used various prepared plants as mouthwash. The tribes were very concerned with oral hygiene. In the Northeast, many tribes such as the Mohegan, Potawatomi, Menominee, and Penobscot used gold thread as floss.

Maria Tallchief, a member of the Osage Nation of Oklahoma, was America's first major prima ballerina. A member of the New York City Ballet, she rose to the top position in 1947.

Thousands of Pueblo Indians live in the southwestern U.S. in New Mexico and Arizona. The most populous of the Pueblo peoples are the Laguna of New Mexico.

Casinos are operated by many tribes in the U.S., the first opened by the Seminoles in Florida. Contrary to popular opinion, the majority of Native nations do not have casinos. Most Native casinos are not profitable. According to the latest figures, only 240 tribes out of 566 had gambling operations, of which 460 were casinos and bingo halls.

It is believed by archaeologists that the Hohokam people of the American Southwest developed the art of etching around A.D. 1000. They used shells as a surface for the etchings and an acid-resistant pitch in which they carved images.

The Cherokee name for Nashville was *Daguna We Lahi* meaning "Mussel Liver Place." No explanation for the name is known.

Most pre-European tribal governments were republics. The tribes had a form of pure democracy in which decisions were reached by consensus.

The first full-blood Native American to become a Catholic priest was Albert Negahuquet, a Potawatomi Indian. He was ordained in the late 1800s.

Modern-day American Indians use beads in arts, crafts, and regalia. Originally, porcupine needles were used for the same purpose.

The Erie Canal in New York is named after the Erie Indians. They were known to other tribes as the Cat Nation. Erie was said to mean "Long Tail" and was a reference to the panther.

In Marin County, California, few people know that the county is named after a chief of the Miwok Indians. This chief, prominent in the early 1800s, lived out his last days at the San Rafael Mission.

Some Native Americans used digging sticks to obtain food from Mother Earth. The stick had a carved pointed end and was used for gathering roots from the soil.

The word *hickory* comes from *Pawcohiccora* from the Powhatan language of Virginia. Hickory is known as good wood for bows.

The Hoop Dance, a breathtaking performance, may use as many as fifty hoops to tell a story. Shapes made by the hoops may represent butterflies, birds, or animals, and the hoop itself depicts the never-ending circle of life. Hoop Dances are performed at pow wows throughout the country.

The Lenni-Lenape (Delaware) who originally lived in New Jersey and Pennsylvania now reside mostly in Oklahoma, Kansas, Wisconsin, and Canada. Some Lenape managed to stay in New Jersey.

Native Americans bathed on a daily basis almost as part of a religious ritual. Cherokees bathed religiously as a part of purification. Some tribal nations in the far north in wintertime, when the rivers were frozen, rolled in the snow for a bath.

The "Talking Stick" is sometimes used at Native American gatherings to allow everyone who so desires to speak, in an orderly manner. In the meeting circle, the stick is passed from one to another, and only the person holding the stick can speak. In U.S. history, it was common for colonists to try to outshout each other at political meetings until Indians taught them a better way.

Contrary to popular belief that Native Americans in the Midwest gathered "wild rice," it was not rice at all, but a type of grass. Also, most of the rice was in fact cultivated in the Great Lakes region for centuries by tribes such as the Ojibwa and Potawatomi. They sowed as much as a third of the crop in the marshes where it was harvested; the rice is still harvested traditionally today.

The traditional headgear for Southeastern Indian men in the 1800s was the turban. An interesting story is that white traders told Natives that since they were being called Indians they should be wearing turbans like East Indians. To be obliging, Native Southerners started wearing turbans— or so the story goes.

Sequoyah and his syllabary

The saying "bury the hatchet" originated with Native Americans. For some tribes when a peace pact was made, there was a literal burying of the hatchet, which was a weapon of war. This practice was first observed by white settlers in New England.

Since the early 1700s, Native leaders were taken to England to meet the King and Queen. England wanted military assistance in its wars against the French in America. The first recorded visits were three Mohawk chiefs and one Mahican in 1710.

Although most tribes were democracies, there were some exceptions. For example, the Natchez who lived in Mississippi had a complex class system, a heredity nobility, and a royal family.

The first Major League American Indian baseball player was Louis Sockalexis of the Penobscot Nation of Maine. He could throw a baseball six hundred feet across the Penobscot River. In 1897 he was selected to play for the Cleveland Spiders, later renamed the Cleveland Indians.

During the 1880s independent Republicans were called *mugwumps*. Little did they know that the term was a Massachusetts Indian word for royalty.

The "bull roarer" is a thin piece of wood about two to three feet long and two to three inches wide. Holes are made in the wood and a cord attached to one end. When it is spun around, it makes a loud roaring sound. It was used by some tribes to bring rain.

Wampum belts were made by Native Americans of purple and white shell beads woven together to record treaties and historic events. Early European colonists also used wampum as money.

The Iroquois Nations, who mostly live in Western New York and Canada, have representatives living in northeastern Oklahoma. The Senecas and Cayugas are descendants of those Iroquois who were living in Ohio in the 1800s.

The American Indian woman considered the most famous basketmaker in the world was Datsolalee, a member of the Washoe tribe of north central California. She lived in the late 1800s and some of her baskets contained more than fifty thousand stitches.

Early Native Americans knew about germs or contagions. In the 1800s, colonists remarked on the tribes' practice of quarantine, isolating people with contagious diseases.

"Indian Iron" was a term given by early European settlers to rawhide made from deerskins. This referred to its tough and amazing resilience when tanned by Native Americans.

The term *cacique*, which comes from Caribbean Arawak Indian origins, is still used by some Pueblo Indian nations for their leaders. The author first encountered modern-day use of the term while working with tribes in the Southwest.

There are no curse words in any Native American language. For example, in Cherokee, the worst term to call anyone is "a dog."

The symbol of Kokopelli, the flute player, is as popular as the dreamcatcher. Kokopelli, originating in the Southwest, is a trickster representing the spirit of music, creativity, and fertility.

The term *caucus* that refers to a political meeting to reach a consensus is from the Algonquin Indian word *cacawaas-sough*, meaning "counselor." It was first used by English colonists in 1773.

North American Indians constructed huge earthen mounds in pyramids for religious and civic purposes. Many of these pyramids were equal in size to those of ancient Egypt. A good example of such earthworks was the Mississippian pyramid city of Cahokia at St. Louis. These mounds were built throughout the East from Michigan to Florida.

Legends tell of a Lost Welsh Colony, led by a Prince Madoc, who predated Columbus's visit to the New World by some three hundred years and intermarried with Native Americans. In the nineteenth century, there stories of Welsh-speaking Indians in the West, but none were ever found.

Many American Indians in olden times did not liked to be photographed, and some in modern times still don't. They referred to cameras as "soul stealers." Protocol at pow wows is that anyone wanting to take a picture of non-performing Natives must always get permission.

The largest pow wow in the U.S. is the Gathering of Nations in Albuquerque, New Mexico. More than 500 tribes from across the U.S. and Canada travel to the huge Gathering every April.

The hunting seasons observed by American sports people and hunters come directly from Native Americans. The Native people taught the European settlers the best time to hunt, taking into account the habits of the animals and the birthing of their young. The settlers had no hunting experience, because in their countries hunting was restricted to royalty.

The Great Law of Peace was the basic tenet of the Haudenosaunee or Iroquois League. The Great Law was written in symbols on wampum belts.

The Adirondack Mountains and National Park in New York are named after the Adirondack Indians who lived in the area. The name is from the Mohawk language and means "Eaters of Bark."

Originally, the Cherokee people observed a thirteen-month year, reflecting that number of phases of the moon. Cherokees adopted the Gregorian or Western calendar year of the mainstream society in the 19th century.

Ancient effigy pottery of Middle Tennessee was carved into shapes such as birds, wolves, dogs, and the like, that could compete with the ceramics of the Glory Days of Rome and Greece.

Stone structures made by ancient Indians called Medicine Wheels can be found in parts of the American West. They were made of a central stone surrounded by a line of stones like spokes on a wagon wheel, and it is thought they served religious purposes. The best known medicine wheel is in the Bighorn National Forest in Wyoming.

Oconaluftee Indian Village is a replica of 1750s Cherokee town, located on the reservation in Cherokee, North Carolina. *Oconaluftee* means "Beside the River." The village, run by the Cherokee Historical Association, portrays Cherokee life in activities such as canoe making, fashioning blowguns, construction of houses, arrowhead making, and more.

Photo by daveynin

Native Americans in old times required little dental care because of the absence of sugar in the foods they consumed. They used the twigs of certain types of bushes, such as the althea, for a type of toothbrush. The use of toothpaste was common to the Northeast and Midwest tribes who dug white clay to care for their teeth. The clay acted as an abrasive and cleaned the teeth as well as polishing them.

The Museum of the Cherokee Indian in Cherokee, N.C., was founded in 1948 by Samuel Beck. It houses the largest collection of Cherokee artifacts in existence. There are thousands of items housed at the museum, with the latest in high-tech presentation of Cherokee creation stories and tribal history plus courses and workshops on authentic methods of arts and crafts.

Cherokees were noted for having the best "country hams" in the South in the late eighteenth century. Southern Indians were credited with the invention of the victual—they had long been smoking venison. Many Cherokees had smokehouses. Settlers traveled to Cherokee towns to barter for the hams, as the chestnut diet of the Indian hogs was said to make the meat the tastiest in the land.

The gripping Cherokee outdoor drama *Unto These Hills* is held from May to August each year in Cherokee, North Carolina. It premiered in 1950 at the Eastern Band of Cherokee Indians Reservation. Millions have attended the drama since its premier. It portrays the history of the Cherokee people from the Desoto expedition in 1540 to the Trail of Tears in 1838.

Eating implements, particularly spoons and forks, abounded among the ancient Indians who lived in the Middle Tennessee region a thousand years ago at a time when the rest of the world was eating with its fingers. There, the first known forks and the first combination spoon and fork—"spork"—made from conch shell originated in the Cumberland Valley, antedating all other such implements made for table use. The four-pronged forks of modern societies were only an invention of the nineteenth century.

The prickly pear cactus is used by American Indians to treat sunburn, rashes, and chapped skin. Some tribal peoples also treated arthritis with cactus pads applied to the affected joints. Oddly enough, although prickly pear grows in the Southeast, it has not been used by Native Americans in that region like it has in Southwest.

In the Mississippian Period of Native American history, a thousand years ago, the area of present-day Nashville, Tennessee, was home to the largest indigenous population in the entire Southeast. Over one million Native inhabitants resided in the Middle Tennessee region in an endless number of towns, villages, and hamlets bustling with a thriving population. There were veritable cities such as Mound Bottom, and other urban enclaves. By the time white settlers arrived in the region in December 1779, it was a shared hunting preserve for the powerful Cherokee Nation and other native tribes. The huge populations had mysteriously disappeared.

Indian influence on the Southern music is best observed in the stomp dance songs of many Southeastern peoples. It has been said that some stomp dance songs sound "bluesy."

The Native diplomats were said to be great orators quite capable of competing with those of Greece or Rome. George Washington was so impressed with the speeches of Ostenaco, a prominent Cherokee leader, that he remarked about the power of his orations although, Washington confessed, he did not understand a word Ostenaco was saying.

According to the most popular story, the Cherokee writing system, the syllabary, was invented by Sequoyah. But according to the traditional Cherokee version of the origin of the syllabary, the writing system is an ancient form of writing, far predating European contact, which had nearly been forgotten but existed among priestly scribes. In this account, Sequoyah revived the writing for the use of all Cherokees as a means of cultural preservation, particularly the Cherokee language.

Pinson Mounds, located about ten miles south of Jackson, Tennessee, is the largest Middle Woodland period site in the Southeast. The ancient city covers four hundred acres, with at least twelve mounds and ancient ritual areas. Pinson Mounds also has the country's tallest mound: Saul's Mound, a burial and ceremonial structure, is seventy-two feet.

In ancient times, huge trade networks connected tribes, nations, and kingdoms from the Great Lakes to the Gulf of Mexico and from Atlantic coast to the foothills of the Rocky Mountains. Native merchants traveling theses networks were perfectly safe and exempt from warfare. Trading was considered a very honorable occupation that could be filled with the adventure of meeting different peoples. A trade language called Mobilian that was based on the Choctaw tongue was the *lingua franca* of the Southeast region.

For thousands of years, Native Americans in the Southern and Eastern Woodlands burned the underbrush in wooded areas in the fall as a means of forest management. This cleared the land for growing grass to attract herds of deer that were hunted for food. Early European explorers described the managed areas as resembling "city parks."

Thin and hollow bird bones were used by Indians of the Eastern Woodlands to make syringes similar to a modern hypodermic needle. The Catawba of South Carolina developed a uniquely tubular syringe with one fitting inside another. The Seneca of New York, using similar techniques, made a disposable baby bottle by washing, drying, and oiling bear intestines and attaching a bird quill by sewing the intestine tightly around it.

Chief Joseph was a leader of the Nez Percé of the Pacific Northwest. He led his tribe against the U.S. Army in the Nez Percé War, a 1,200-mile fighting retreat in 1877. He's best known for his words at surrender: "I will fight no more forever." The conflict gained world renown for the tribe and Chief Joseph, who became known as a peacemaker and humanitarian.

Several hundred years ago Native surgeons in North, Central, and South America were performing delicate and complex operations using anesthetics and antibiotics. In North America, Native healers used sutures of human hair to close wounds and incisions. Throughout the Americas, razor-sharp scalpels were made of flint, chert, or obsidian.

"Chiggers" is the name Southerners give to tiny mites that can be agonizingly itchful. The name comes from *chigoes*, a term for mites that comes from the Carib Indian language of the Caribbean.

The main ingredient for tabasco sauce is chilies cultivated by American Indians thousands of years ago. A Choctaw cook developed a brand of hot sauce, "Hotter 'n Hell," that can well compete with the hottest tabasco.

Many ancient Native North American cities, such as Cahokia and those of Hopewell cultures in the Midwest as well as Pinson Mounds in West Tennessee, were laid out according to astronomical events. Those urban centers had perfectly aligned streets with residential areas and ceremonial buildings.

The name *Tennessee* is derived from the name of the ancient Cherokee town of Tanase in the eastern part of the state. Tanase was, in the early eighteenth century, the leading town of the Cherokee Nation until it was surpassed by nearby Chota in population and influence. Chota was at one time an outskirt town of Tanase. As Chota grew, the former capital faded out of existence or was absorbed by its suburb.

Although most accounts state that the celebrated Sequoyah died and was buried in Mexico in 1843, there is another more mysterious story. Noted Oklahoma Cherokee author Jack F. Kilpatrick reports that according to a manuscript in the Cherokee syllabary written in the 1840s and found at Lake Tenkiller in eastern Oklahoma in the 1960s, Sequoyah was "lost" by the two young men accompanying him on his trip in northern Mexico, one of whom was his son Tessee. They went to hunt for food and left the elderly Sequoyah in a cave to rest. When they returned, he was gone and his tracks abruptly disappeared. They searched from him for four days. In their words, "We lost Sequoyah."

The term "caucus" that most often refers to a political meeting to reach a consensus is from the Algonquin Indian word, *cacawaassough,* with the same meaning.

In 1492, more than three hundred Indian languages were spoken in what is now the United States. The largest language families were the Algonquian, Muskhogean, Iroquoian, Siouan, and Uto-Aztecan. Today more than one hundred languages are still spoken by present-day Native Americans. Some tribes have only a handful of speakers; others have thousands. The Navaho Nation is first in language retention.

Sassafras tea was drunk with meals by most tribes in the South. The roots of the tree were boiled to make the tea. Sassafras was also consumed in the spring to condition the body for summer heat.

The Chinook Indians of Washington lived in large cedar plank houses. Each roomy dwelling could provide a home for several families.

Poke salad (or poke sallet) was a staple vegetable eaten by both Native Americans and settlers in the Southeast. In Middle Tennessee it was often called Shawnee sallet in memory of that tribe that once lived in the area. The name *poke* comes from the Virginia Algonquian word for the plant, *Pokan*.

The Eastern Cherokees of the Eastern Band of Cherokee Indians have the longest continuing pottery tradition, stretching back nearly two thousand years, of any tribes in the U.S. still in their original homeland. Ancient Cherokee potters made stamped pottery that was thin-walled and waterproof. The Cherokee Potters Guild was established to carry on this age-old ceramic tradition following workshops at the Museum of the Cherokee Indian in 2003.

Native Americans chewed milkweed as chewing gum; they chewed the hardened sap of plants such as licorice, marshmallow, and hollyhock to sweeten breath and relieve hunger and thirst. American Indians in the Northeast taught colonists to chew spruce sap as a breath freshener, and by the early 1800s spruce gum became the first commercial chewing gum.

Indian children were provided with a wide variety of toys, including the spinning top and the whirligig. Dolls were also used as well as kites, stilts, and miniature bows and arrows.

Many authorities believe that the Siouan people of the Dakotas originally lived on the south Atlantic seaboard and the Gulf Coast. Many of the coastal tribes spoke Siouan including the present-day Catawba of South Carolina.

Stickball, a cultural ancestor of the game of lacrosse, is called *Anetsa* in Cherokee and is referred to as the "Little War." The rough game combines elements of football, basketball, baseball, track, boxing, and wrestling.

Lacrosse, called the fastest game on two feet, was a sport played in various forms by Native Americans from the Great Lakes and the Northeast to the Deep South. The Iroquois nations who live in New York and Canada called the game *baggataway*.

Many Indian peoples before the development of fire resistant pottery brought ingredients to a boil by dropping heated clay balls into water held in waterproof baskets. Heated clay balls were also used in a type of oven covered with leaves and stones.

Red Cloud was chief of the Oglala Lakoa from 1868 to 1989. Recognized as one of the most capable Native war leaders, he fought Red Cloud's War against the U.S. Army over control of parts of Wyoming and Montana.

Although this fact is not well known to most, thousands of Native Americans fought in the Civil War. In fact a total of over 28,000 fought in the conflict on both sides. All tribes east of the Mississippi with the exception of the Florida Seminoles were involved. In Oklahoma, all of the removed Southern and Eastern tribes lined up for either the Union or the Confederacy. Among the Western Cherokees, a tribal civil war erupted with Union and Confederate Cherokee regiments. Confederate Cherokee General Stand Watie was the last Southern officer to surrender.

Cherokee dugout canoes came in three types. A racing canoe was twelve to fifteen feet long. A traveling canoe was used for transporting people and goods. Last but not least, the war canoe was for moving warriors on military maneuvers.

Potato chips were invented in the nineteenth century by a Native American in New York. George Crum, Mohawk, was a cook at a fancy resort in Saratoga Springs. In the summer of 1853, wealthy railroad magnate Cornelius Vanderbilt, dining at the resort, complained that the French fries were too thick and sent them back. Crum fried another order, which was also sent back. By then, an angry Crum shaved the potatoes into paper-thin slices to spite the finicky Vanderbilt, again fried them, and sent them to the table. Vanderbilt was delighted with the culinary novelty; potato chips became in vogue for the uppercrust set and were sold throughout the Northeast. Crum later opened his own restaurant serving the treat originally made in anger.

The state of Iowa gets its name from the Iowa Tribe that lived in the lands. The name means "One Who Puts To Sleep."

Qualla Arts and Crafts, on the Eastern Band of Cherokee Indians Reservation, houses the largest collection of authentic Cherokee art on the reservation. All of the artists whose works are displayed for sale are enrolled members of the Eastern Band of Cherokee.

Throughout North, Central, and South America, Native Americans used astronomical observations to create calendars for a number of reasons, including determining the start of the planting seasons. At Cahokia, a huge ancient urban center of the Mississippian culture built near present-day St. Louis, a calendaric structure called "Woodhenge" was aligned to the position of the sun at equinoxes and solstices for agricultural purposes. The ancient Maya devised a lunar calendar that was more accurate than any other in the world at that time.

The freedom afforded women in the Iroquois culture was used as a model for the women's movement in the U.S. in the early twentieth century. Iroquois society is matrilineal and hold the woman in high esteem with freedoms equal to men.

There is much doubt and little to support the story of Pocahontas saving the life of Captain John Smith as he was about to be executed by her tribe, the Powhatan. In fact, Smith made no mention of such an incident while in America. He wrote the account in an autobiography years after he returned to England. Speculation is that he manufactured the story to sell the book.

There is the somewhat doubtful story of Indians selling Manhattan Island for twenty-four dollars. In all probability the Natives may have given the colonists simply the right to hunt and fish on the island. But even more likely was that the twenty-four dollars in beads was merely looked upon as establishing friendship between the Indians and the newcomers. This seems most probable in light of this writer's knowledge of Native custom, protocol, and history.

The term *barbecue* comes from the Taino Indians of the Caribbean, who introduced the practice of cooking meat in this fashion. This open-fire cooking method was called *barbacoa*, from which the current word is derived.

Stones shaped like round discs were used in an popular ancient game. Stones for the game of Chunky were made with painstaking care, perfectly fashioned with a high-gloss polish comparable to modern machine finishes. Players rolled a stone and tried to land his spear nearest it.

Yansa, the name for *buffalo,* is basically the same in all Southern Indian tongues: in Cherokee, *Yansa*; in Choctaw, *Yannash;* in Creek, *Yvnvsv* (*v* is pronounced a nasal short vowel "unh"). An ancient tradition says that originally all Native people spoke the same language.

Native Americans in the Southeast taught colonists to make fried corn bread by dropping spoonfuls of rolled corn dough into hot bear fat. The result—*voilà*—hushpuppies!

Most tribes, in fact all tribes with which this writer is familiar, reject the Bering Strait theory of Native American origins. All from Cherokee to Sioux, from Ottawa to Choctaw, from Apache to Mohawk, all have creation and migration stories of having originated in the Western Hemisphere. If anything, humans migrated from this hemisphere to all other parts of the world and not the reverse.

Despite a common image from television of Indians attacking wagon trains, this rarely occurred. Most of the time Plains peoples avoided the covered wagon caravans because they were afraid of contagious diseases.

The Desoto expedition of 1540 encountered not just tribes and confederacies, but veritable Native kingdoms with elaborate pomp and ceremony reminiscent of ancient Egypt. A good example was the Queen of Cofitachiqui, who was carried around on a litter complete with litter-bearers.

The swastika, a symbol long present in Southwestern Native American culture on baskets and pottery, has disappeared from most Native art because of its use by Adolf Hitler to represent Nazism. A federal government petition signed by the Hopi, Apache, and Tohono O'odham during World War II pledged not to use the swastika in any art and crafts.

The name *Mississippi* is derived from the Algonquian word *MiciSibi* meaning "Big River." A French map of 1695 brought the name into current use.

American Indians in the Northern and Southern woodlands boiled willow bark to make a tea containing salicylic acid, the active ingredient in aspirin. This tea was a pain reliever, a fever reducer, and an anti-inflammatory. Indians shared the knowledge with early colonists.

A legendary Cherokee keeper of tradition, Walker Calhoun, lived his entire life in the Big Cove community of the Eastern Band of Cherokee Indians reservation. He dedicated his life to preserving the languages, traditions, and lore of the Cherokee people for future generations. From his own family he formed the Raven Rock Dancers to hold and share traditional dances. In 1988, at a meeting of the Eastern and Western Cherokee, he received the Sequoyah Award for his lifelong contributions.

Ancient Native Americans performed brain surgery, conducting a medical procedure that surgically removed parts of the skull to eliminate disease or to relieve trauma to the brain. Evidence of this procedure has been found in ancient skulls in several regions of the U.S. and Canada. The most abundant evidence of brain surgery has been found in what is now Peru. The survival rate of patients in that area was eighty to ninety percent.

The Ojibwa of the Great Lakes performed a type of plastic surgery. They could repair torn ears. They would trim the ear tissue so that both sides of the tear matched up evenly and then suture them together.

The word *chipmunk* has is origin in the Odawa (Ottawa) language. It is *jidamoonh* in Odawa, meaning "red squirrel."

Jay Silverheels was a Mohawk Indian actor born on the Six Nations Reserve of the Grand River First Nation in Ontario, Canada. He was the original Tonto in the *Lone Ranger* television series of the 1950s. Silverheels was a spokesperson for Native American actors and founded the Indian Actors Workshop in 1966.

As Cherokee women had so much authority and freedom in government and everyday life, British colonists remarked that the Cherokees lived under a "petticoat government." There was a War Women's Council, and Beloved Women could decide the fate of war captives with just the wave of a swan's wing. Also, some women fought in the war companies alongside the men.

The environmental movement was started by the teachings of Native Americans. During the 1960s many young non-Indians, dubbed "hippies," were looking for answers to increased pollution and other environmental destruction and turned to American Indians for solutions. They visited with Hopi elder Thomas Banyaca, and from his teachings was started the observance of Earth Day.

Some things come about by happenstance. Good example: the Native American Graves Protection and Repatriation Act. In the summer of 1986 a Northern Cheyenne delegation visiting Washington, D.C., toured the Smithsonian's Cheyenne collection. They saw the room with huge ceilings that contained row upon row of drawers. A delegate remarked there must be a lot of "Indian stuff" in the drawers. A curator matter-of-factly said, "Oh, this is where we keep skeletal remains"—about 18,500 ancestors. The delegation was shocked. They spread the word, and this discovery started a national Indian movement that brought about NAGPRA.

Clay salt pans were used by ancient Indians in Middle Tennessee. These salt pans were pottery in which water from the salt licks was allowed to evaporate, leaving behind the precious commodity.

Despite the name "Irish potatoes," all of these tuber-producing plants are native to the Americas. This plant originated in the Andes Mountains of South America in about 8000 B.C. The potato found its way north in pre-contact days. The Spaniards took the tuber to Europe.

Sunflowers were first cultivated by American Indians in Arizona and New Mexico around 3000 B.C. With extensive trade networks, by 200 B.C. sunflowers were raised all over the southern and eastern woodlands.

The ancient Indians of Middle Tennessee ingeniously made fish hooks from the bones of deer toes. The hooks, while appearing fragile, were strong and have withstood the ravages of time as some have been found in caves.

Joy Harjo, an Muscogee Creek author, poet, screenwriter, and musician from Tulsa, Oklahoma, is the author of numerous books and poems. Harjo has received such honors as the American Indian Achievement Award, the PEN Open Book Award, the Josephine Miles Poetry Award, and the William Carlos Williams Award.

The Dover Flint Quarries in Stewart County, Tennessee, were the source of the beautiful flint that ancient Native Americans in the South used to carve exquisite ceremonial objects. This flint was highly prized because it could be mined in large sheets that could be worked into long, slender blades of various shapes, including swords and maces. The Dover Flint Quarries were placed in the National Register of Historic Places in 1993.

Cherokee chiefs were first taken to England and treated royally in the 1730s. Among those who went over the years were Attakullakulla, Stalking Turkey, Pouting Pigeon, and Ostenaco. Cherokee leaders generally had quite a time socializing in Great Britain; there were even poems written about them.

Squanto is best remembered in history as the Indian who came to the aid of the English colonists in Massachusetts in 1621. What is not commonly known is that he was part of a group of bodyguards to the chiefs of his tribe. He was a Patuxet Indian, and a member of the warrior elite. In 1614 he was kidnapped by English sailors and sold into slavery in Europe. Squanto made it back to America before the Pilgrims arrived in 1620 and surprised them by speaking English with a British accent!

Ice and field hockey are based on the American Indian game Shinny, which was played mostly by women. The modern name, *hockey*, is from the French word *hocquet,* a shepherd's crook, which resembled the sticks of the Native players.

Fringed clothing thought by many to serve as decoration also had a very functional purpose. It was believed by Native people that fringe drained water from garments in rainy weather.

Hopi Indian Lewis Tewanima was a U.S. two-time Olympic silver medalist and long-distance runner. Tewanima is a legendary runner to the Hopi Nation. His silver medal record stood unbroken for fifty-two years. He was a teammate of the great Olympic athlete, Jim Thorpe of the Sac and Fox Nation.

Sitting Bull was a Lakota holy man who became a chief to resist the U.S. government. Following a vision in which he saw a major victory, he inspired his tribe to defeat General George Armstrong Custer and the 7th Cavalry at the Battle of the Little Bighorn in 1876. After his later surrender he performed with Buffalo Bill's Wild West Show.

The ingredients in the first soft drinks came directly from Native Americans, including vanilla, sarsaparilla, sassafras, winter-green, and birch. Sarsaparilla was used in root beer. Because of the bitter taste from many herbal ingredients in early soft drinks, these beverages were often called peppers. In fact, this is how Dr Pepper got its name.

Peanut butter, the tasty treat enjoyed around the world, owes its origin to ancient Indians. It was invented hundreds of years ago by the Incas of Peru. The peanut is a native plant of South America and is believed to have originated in Brazil. Ancient peoples obtained the plant from Brazil and were growing peanuts as early as 3900 B.C. to 2500 B.C. In the 1500s, Portuguese exported peanuts to Asia and West Africa.

The Indian head nickel is not the head of one Indian, but three. The profile is a composite of three western Native Americans: Big Tree (Kiowa), Two Moons (Cheyenne), and Iron Tail (Sioux). The three Native leaders were photographed on a visit to President Theodore Roosevelt by sculptor James Earle Fraser.

Image courtesy of CCF Numismatics

A cradle board is a baby carrier that allowed an Indian woman to do her work while watching her child be safe, content, and inactive. Eastern Woodland mothers would strap their infants snugly into soft leather pouches attached to wooden frames a few weeks after birth. Dried moss was used to keep the baby dry and comfortable.

The modern science of ecology, developed in the mid-1990s, owes a debt to the thinking of Native Americans. Indians always believed in preserving the natural environment. For example, when gathering herbal plants, only every fourth one is picked for use.

The state name *Arkansas* comes from a word in the language of the Illinois Indians meaning "Down River People" or "Down-Stream People," said to refer to a now-extinct tribe.

Native Americans invented string games long before contact with non-Indians. For example, the Cat's Cradle, a string game of making figures by looping string on the fingers, was played by many Southeastern tribes.

The Constitution of the Iroquois Confederacy, The Six Nations, made such a political impression on the colonists that many including Benjamin Franklin suggested it be a model for the Articles of Confederation, which were the basis for the U.S. Constitution. The federal system of government is based on the Iroquois Constitution.

All tribes had midwives responsible for helping pregnant women with delivery. They were usually medicine women, an honored position in Native American societies.

The Wampanoag of Massachusetts worked in the whaling industry in the nineteenth century, sailing around the world. In ancient times, the Wampanoag hunted the huge sea creatures in small kayak-like boats. In the 1850s, Amos Hoskins of the Aquinnah band of the Wampanoag was the captain of his own whaling ship, *Massasoit,* named after the chief who welcomed the Pilgrims.

Wes Studi is a prominent Oklahoma Cherokee actor. He has appeared in such Academy Award-winning films as *Dances with Wolves, The Last of the Mohicans,* and *Geronimo: An American Legend.* Studi is the second Native American inducted into the National Cowboy and Western Heritage Museum's Hall of Great Western Performers. He also serves as honorary chair of the Indigenous Language Institute.

Adobe, now used extensively in home construction in the southwestern U.S., was developed by the Pueblo tribes around 3000 B.C. This building material is perfect for the hot, dry climate as it keeps dwellings cool in the highest temperatures.

The name *Illinois* is that of a Native Confederacy composed of several tribes: the Kaskaskia, Cahokia, Michigamea, Moingwena, Tamaroa, and Peoria. The two surviving tribes, the Kaskaskia and Peoria, removed to Oklahoma in the early nineteenth century. *Illinois* means "Warrior" or "Man."

A popular snack today, jerky was invented by the Northern Plains Indians, who dried buffalo meat after cutting it into strips and smoking it over a fire. Jerky could last for up to three years. How's that for non-refrigerated food preservation!

Contrary to popular belief, not all Indians wore buckskin and moccasins. In the Southeast, many tribes made cloth from the inner bark of the mulberry tree. Some people such as the Cherokee made feather cloaks out of turkey feathers. Other tribes made slippers from the fiber of a yucca-type plant. In the 1880s a twined slipper estimated to be several hundred years old was found in the Salts Cave in Kentucky.

Over many decades Mohawk Indian ironworkers have been building skyscrapers in New York. These dauntless construction workers were key in raising the Empire State Building, the George Washington Bridge, the Rockefeller Trade Center, the Waldorf Astoria, and many others. High-rise work has been a tradition among Mohawks since the mid-1800s.

In the 1930s and 1940s, American Indian art was a huge influence and inspiration on the modern American abstract art movement. Reflecting on Native Art from the Arctic Circle to South America, art historians view these works as advanced, sophisticated, and powerful. Many artists such as Jackson Pollock, who was raised in the West, borrowed themes from Native art in his early career.

In the world of rap, Native Americans have also set their moccasin print. The Cherokee rapper Gary Davis, aka Litefoot, performs inspirational Indian rap on reservations across the country. He has been a frequent performer at the Cherokee Indian Fair in Western North Carolina. Litefoot is also an actor, most famously starring in *Indian in the Cupboard.*

The Comanche, called "the Lords of the Southern Plains," also spoke a language related to the Aztec tongue. The Comanche were Plains Indians living in teepees, whereas the Aztecs were rulers of Mexico living in great ornate cities. There is a lot to be said for location, location, location!

Bud Adams, late owner of the Tennessee Titans NFL franchise, was an enrolled member of the Cherokee Nation of Oklahoma. Over the years, Adams was very supportive of the Cherokee National Historical Society, having funded Adams's Corner, the nineteenth-century Cherokee village in Tahlequah, Oklahoma.

Many of the Southeastern tribes, particularly Cherokees, made beautiful capes of turkey feathers. These cloaks were warm in winter and dry in rainy weather.

The remaining ceremonial and burial mounds of the ancient Indian metropolis Cahokia, a veritable city with a population of over 30,000, are located just outside of St. Louis. It was so large that there was a downtown Cahokia with suburbs and neighborhoods organized around urban plazas. Huge earthworks remain, including Monk's Mound standing about one hundred feet high; its the top is nearly as large as a football field and held a structure around five thousand square feet.

Strawberries were highly regarded by Southeastern peoples as a tasty fruit. In Cherokee lore, strawberries were responsible for bringing the First Woman, Selu, and the First Man, Kanati, back together after their first argument.

The Mississippi Band of Choctaw Indians in 2013 acquired seventy-nine acres of land in West Tennessee that has been placed in Federal Indian Trust status. This is the first reservation land in the state in 175 years. There has been a Choctaw community in West Tennessee since the 1950s.

The Eastern Band of Cherokee Indians Reservation is the only federally recognized tribal trust area in the state of North Carolina. It is composed of the main reservation of 55,000 acres and other tracts at Snowbird near Robbinsville.

The Central Arizona Project, which provides water to Phoenix, uses many of the same canals developed by the Hohokam people thousands of years ago. The canals, several feet deep, were filled with concrete in modern times to prevent water seepage.

The oldest duck decoys in the world have been found in northwest Utah. The duck decoy was invented by Native Americans about three thousand years ago. It is thought the inventors were the ancestors of the Paiute people.

The *Trail of Tears* drama sponsored by the Cherokee Nation of Oklahoma picks up where *Unto These Hills* leaves off, portraying Cherokee history from the arrival of Cherokees in the West, through the Civil War, and ending with the formation of the state of Oklahoma in 1907.

Parched corn was as common to Southern Indians as bread is to today's folk. It was fixed by throwing kernels of corn on a heated flattened stone, a handful at a time, which were rolled around until roasted. The roasted kernels were pounded in a wooden mortar into corn meal.

Will Rogers, a famous Cherokee humanist and philosopher from Oologah Indian Territory, now known as Claremore, Oklahoma, is considered the father of late-night humor. He was the first humorist to use material from national politics in his comedy.

Chucalissa is a reconstructed Indian village on an ancient site in T.O. Fuller Park in Memphis, Tennessee. Located on a bluff overlooking the Mississippi River, the large Mississippian town complete with ceremonial grounds was occupied from about 1000 to 1500 CE. In recent years it has been the site of modern-day pow wows. The C.H. Nash Museum includes numerous exhibits and a hands-on archaeology laboratory.

Running was a very important component of pre-contact Native American life, as the relay method was used to send messages from village to village and tribe to tribe. Native couriers were the main means of transmitting information. One eighteenth-century Iroquois runner, Sharp Shins, was renowned for covering ninety to a hundred miles in one day.

Will Sampson was a renowned Muscogee Creek Indian actor born in Okmulgee, Oklahoma. His first notable role was as Chief Bromen in *One Flew over the Cuckoo's Nest*. Sampson also starred in *Fish Hawk, The Outlaw Josey Wales, Orca,* and *Poltergeist*. He was also a noted artist. Sampson was an advocate of realistic depictions of American Indians in movies.

The Inuit (Eskimo) of Alaska have dozens of words for snow. As snow is such a constant part of the environment, minute descriptions could be critical to survival. A few of the words for different types of snow are *patuqun* (frosty, sparkling snow), *apun* (fallen snow), *mahak* (melting snow), *apiqun* (first snow in autumn), and *aniu* (good snow to make drinking water).

Moccasin styles were often so unique that the tribe of the person could sometimes be known just by the track of the footwear. Moccasins of some nations had fringes on the heels. The word *moccasin* is from the Narragansett tribe of Rhode Island.

The state name *Missouri* is the Algonquian word for "Muddy Water." It is also the name of a tribe that now lives in North Central Oklahoma.

The most important food animal to Native Americans in the Southeast was the abundant white-tailed deer, while Plains dwellers relied on buffalo. These animals provided most of the meat consumed, plus skin for clothes, moccasins, blankets, and bedding.

Scurvy, a disease caused by a Vitamin C deficiency, rarely afflicted Native Americans. If it occurred, they had a ready cure which they shared with early European explorers, Vitamin C-rich foods.

In Florida, early American Indians built seawalls by stacking up enormous quantities of shells. One seawall was more than ten feet high, composed mainly of conch shells. These seawalls protected the coastlines from erosion by ocean waves.

Some twenty-six states in the United States have American Indian-derived names. There are also countless numbers of cities, rivers, lakes, counties, and mountains with names of Native American origin.

Among famous jazz trombonists of the twentieth century was Russell Moore, a Pima Indian. He was called "Big Chief" in music circles. From an early age Moore studied piano, drums, French horn, and trombone. In the 1930s he played with Lionel Hampton and in the 1940s with Louis Armstrong's band. He toured the U.S. and Canada in his career.

Pumpkins were domesticated by Native American farmers thousands of years ago. They boiled or roasted pumpkins, and also roasted and ate the seeds. The next time pumpkin pie is served at the dinner table, remember where it started!

The state name *Wisconsin* is from the Ojibwa language meaning "Gathering of Waters" or "Grassy Place." The term was first used on maps by the French in 1695.

Chief "Powhatan," mistakenly named by the English after his village, is known for capturing Captain John Smith of Jamestown. Powhatan was the father of Pocahontas. In 1608 Captain Christopher Newport tried to crown Powhatan to make him an English servant. The ceremony ended when Powhatan refused to kneel.

An Aleut word *Alyeska,* meaning "mainland" or "great land" led to the name *Alaska.* Some linguists believe it came from an Inuit word *Alayxsa,* also meaning "mainland." Since Aleut and Inuit are related languages, both positions could be right.

The Nez Percé Indians of Idaho are credited with developing the strong, sure-footed breed of Appaloosa horse. They selectively bred these horses for speed and intelligence through careful mating. It is said that Appaloosa are so sure-footed that they can climb mountain trails almost like mountain sheep.

Utah is a term given by the White Mountain Apache to the Navaho (Dineh) meaning "Those Farther Up." The Spanish thought it also referred to the Utes.

	a	e	i	o	u	v [ə]
	D a	R e	T i	Ꭳ o	O u	i v
	Ꮝ ga Ꮙ ka	F ge	y gi	A go	J gu	E gv
	Ꮙ ha	P he	Ꮧ hi	Ꮏ ho	Γ hu	Ꮆ hv
	W la	Ꮩ le	P li	G lo	M lu	Ꮑ lv
	Ꮉ ma	Ꮕ me	H mi	Ꮠ mo	y mu	
	Θ na Ꮏ hna G nah	Ꮑ ne	h ni	Z no	Ꮕ nu	Ꮓ nv
	Ꮖ qua	Ꮗ que	Ꮘ qui	Ꮖ quo	Ꮘ quu	Ꮞ quv
	Ꭶ s Ꮜ sa	4 se	b si	Ꮢ so	Ꮧ su	R sv
	Ꮣ da W ta	S de Ꮦ te	Ꮧ di Ꮨ ti	Ꭺ do	S du	Ꮫ dv
	Ꮬ dla Ꮭ tla	L tle	C tli	Ꮴ tlo	Ꮵ tlu	P tlv
	G tsa	V tse	Ꮶ tsi	K tso	Ꮪ tsu	C tsv
	G wa	Ꮺ we	Θ wi	Ꮼ wo	9 wu	6 wv
	Ꮿ ya	ß ye	Ꮅ yi	Ꮆ yo	G yu	B yv

With the spread of what is called the Sequoyah syllabary, the Cherokee of Oklahoma became more literate than any of the neighboring non-Indian populations, achieving more than ninety percent literacy within one year. Between 1835 and 1861, over nearly fourteen million pages of books, pamphlets, tracts, and passages from the Bible were printed in the Cherokee writing system. Cherokee achievements were incredible!

Medicine pills were nothing new to some Eastern Woodland Indians who ground moist cranberry bark and shaped it into pills. Early colonists called it "cramp bark" since Indians used its pain-reducing qualities to treat menstrual cramps.

The U.S. Native American population is generally considered as being undercounted. In 2010 the official figure was 2.5 million, but the real number was estimated at 2.9 million. Guess about 400,000 Natives are hiding out somewhere.

Most major U.S. cities have American Indian Centers for urban Indian populations. Indian centers were largely the result of the U.S. government's relocation policy of the 1950s to assimilate Indians into the mainstream. Just the opposite happened. The Chicago American Indian Center started in 1953.

The Iroquois and Hurons in the Northeast and the Cherokees in the Southeast frequently fortified their border towns with stockades of timbers set in the ground. These walls were complete with watchtowers and platforms for defensive purposes. The European explorers were so impressed with the stockades that they referred to the towns as castles.

In the Southeast, Native people ate fresh persimmons and made them into drinks. But don't eat persimmons until after the first frost, because you do, it will pucker your mouth. Hence the Cherokee name *tsa la lui,* which means "pucker mouth."

Tobacco, while used by Native Americans for ceremonial purposes, was also used for healing. Among Cherokees insect bites were treated with moist tobacco applied to the sting.

The state *Massachusetts* is named after the Massachusett tribe. The tribe's descendants still live in the Greater Boston area organized as the Massachusetts-Ponkapoag Tribal Council. The names comes from an Algonquian word meaning "Large Hill Place" or "At the Hill."

Born in Norman, Oklahoma, famed guitarist Jesse Ed Davis was Muscogee Creek, Seminole, and Kiowa. He played country western, rock, and jazz with such greats as Conway Twitty, Willie Nelson, Taj Mahal, Rod Stewart, and Eric Clapton. In 2002, he was inducted into the Oklahoma Jazz Hall of Fame.

Native Americans on reservations do not pay state taxes, but are still subject to federal income tax. The tribes do not levy taxes on their members.

A gigantic animal-shaped monolith thought to have been carved by ancient Indians astonished early settlers in Putnam County, Tennessee. It was described as a big dog in a sitting position. Colonists referred to it as the "Standing Stone."

Rodney Grant, an Omaha Indian actor, is probably best known for playing the Lakota warrior "Wind in His Hair" in Dances with Wolves. He also appeared in a host of other films including *Geronimo: An American Legend*, *War Party*, and *Powwow Highway*. Grant also portrayed "Chingachcook" in the television series *Hawkeye* in the 1990s.

Native Americans have contributed hundreds of words to the English language. Some words of native origin are *hubbub*, *peewee*, *raccoon*, *papoose*, *woodchuck*, and even *Yankee*!

Famous Native Americans

Edmondia Lewis, artist • **Susan Picotte,** doctor • **Russell Means,** activist •
Jim Thorpe, athlete • **Squanto,** Pilgrims' friend • **Sacagawea,** explorer •
Pocahantas • **Rita Coolidge,** singer • **Wayne Newton,** singer •
Maria TallChief, ballerina • **Hiawatha,** religious figure • **Sequoyah,** inventor •
Wilma Mankiller, women's rights activist • **Dr. Carlos Montezuma,** physician •
Sarah Winnemucca, journalist • **Will Rogers,** humorist • **Billy Mills,** athlete •
Charles Curtis, U.S. vice president •
Buffy Sainte-Marie, actor •
Jay Silverheels, actor

LEADERS AND WARRIORS
**Black Hawk, Chief Joseph,
Cochise, Crazy Horse, Geronimo,
Nancy Ward, Pontiac, Powhatan,
Red Cloud, Sitting Bull, Tecumseh**

Hattie Kaufman, formerly a national news correspondent with the CBS *Early Show,* was the first and only Native American to work for a national network. She is from the Nez Percé Reservation in Idaho.

N. Scott Momaday is a much-celebrated Native American writer of the Kiowa Nation. His best-known work, *House Made of Dawn,* was awarded the Pulitzer Prize in 1969. Momaday has been called the Founding Father of the Native American Renaissance.

Breastplates and chokers that are worn as part of regalia have their origin as body armor. The breastplate was to protect the chest from arrows and the choker protected the throat area.

Jim Thorpe

There are fifty or more tribal towns in the Muscogee Creek Nation of Oklahoma. This is equal to fifty tribes in the Creek Nation. Just like having fifty states in the Union.

Three Cherokee Nations are recognized by the federal government: the Cherokee Nation of Oklahoma, the United Keetoowah Band of Cherokee Indians (also in Oklahoma), and the Eastern Band of Cherokee Indians in North Carolina. The three Cherokee entities are the result of the removal policies of the 1830s.

Ancient Native cities, urban areas, and earthen mounds show complex knowledge of geometry. Cahokia, Moundville, Etowah, and other Indian metropolises required advanced mathematics in their construction.

In the Northeastern Woodlands, the Wampanoag and neighboring tribes used fish as fertilizer. The fish, menhaden, was not used for food. In the Southeast, the soil was so fertile that fertilizer was not needed.

The Northeast Native Nations ate popcorn by the handful and also made it into soup. Some tribes even used popcorn ceremonially as a goodwill offering in peace negotiations with British colonists.

Native Americans of the Poverty Point culture in what is now Louisiana made briquettes for cooking in 600 B.C. The briquettes were heated until red-hot. Then hundreds of them were placed in a roasting pit with the food, covered and cooked as in a modern-day oven.

Dave Anderson, the founder of the Famous Dave's Restaurant chain, is a Choctaw/Ojibwa Indian. Born in Chicago, he grew up there and on reservations in Wisconsin. He is a former Assistant Secretary of Indian Affairs and is the author of several award-winning books.

The site of the ancient Cherokee town of Kituhwa outside of Bryson City, North Carolina, is where the first Cherokee town in the Southeast stood. From this sacred town originated all Cherokees in the South. To this day many Cherokees call themselves *Ani-Kituhwa*, meaning people of the Kituhwa.

The Muscogee Creeks of Alabama and Georgia prepared corn in at least forty-two ways. How's that for creativity in cooking!

The Cherokee Indian Fair celebrated its hundredth anniversary in October 2012 at the Eastern Band of Cherokee Indians reservation. Thousands of Cherokees and non-Cherokees attended the week-long fair in Cherokee, North Carolina.

Like most tribes, Cherokee did not originally refer themselves by that name. The original tribal name is *Ani-Yunwiya or Ani-Kituhwa*.

There are many federally recognized tribes without reservations, mostly in Oklahoma. Thirty-nine recognized tribes reside in the state, but no reservations. All reservations in Oklahoma were disestablished when the state was admitted to the Union in 1907.

The first Indian-constructed hospital was that of the Choctaw Nation of Oklahoma, which had its own funding in the 1990s. It receives 150,000 to 210,000 outpatient visits per year.

Cherokee is an Iroquoian language, or it could be said Iroquois is a Cherokeean language (remember it's in Cherokee). Cherokee is an ancient language, and studies have found that the two languages separated over 3,500 years ago.

The Calusa Indians of Florida built large stone enclosures to hold fish and other water creatures for food. They never had to worry about fresh fish.

Some say Michigan gets its name from the Ojibwa words *Mici and Gami* meaning "Big Water." Others believe it is from the Ojibwa *Mizhiigan*, for "Cut-Over Clearing."

Robert Conley is a prolific Cherokee author and a member of the United Keetoowah Band of Cherokee Indians. He has written more than fifty books, mostly on Cherokee historical fiction themes. In 2007 Conley received the Lifetime Achievement Award from the Native Writers Circle of the Americas.

The first Native movie star is considered Lillian St. Cyr, a member of the Ho-Chunk Nation. She appeared in sixty-five films beginning in 1908 as Princess Red Wing. Another early the earliest American Indian actor was a Seneca called Chief John Bigtree, whose career began in 1917.

The Jena Band of Choctaw Indian, based in Central Louisiana, are one of three federally recognized Choctaw tribes in the United States. The Jena Band were granted federal recognition in 1995. In the early 1900s the Jena Band of Choctaw walked to Oklahoma, but later walked back to Louisiana after changing their minds about relocating to Oklahoma.

Harpoons were long ago used by Native Americans on the Northwest Coast for hunting whales. The Nootka and Mohah people hunted whales with detachable pointed harpoons and floats.

Popcorn poppers were invented by Native Americans in the southwestern U.S. The popper, made of pottery, was filled with heated sand, melted animal fat, and corn kernels. The popper was shaken until popcorn was ready to eat.

The Native American love of music continues to resonate with contemporary American Indians. Some of the great Native musicians in various genres are Buffy Sainte-Marie (Cree), Joanne Shenandoah (Iroquois), Jim Pepper (Muscogee Creek/Kaw), Bill Miller (Mahican), Robert Mirabal (Taos Pueblo), Jesse Ed Davis (Muscogee Creek/Seminole–Kiowa), Litefoot (Cherokee Nation), Robbie Robertson (Mohawk), Redbone (Mission Indians), R. Carlos Nakai (Navajo/Ute) and Keith Secola (Ojibwa).

The Kiowa language is in the Uto-Aztecan language family, the same family that includes Nahuatl, the tongue of the Aztecs. This means the Kiowas (originally from Montana, now based in Oklahoma) and the Aztecs (from central Mexico) were at one time the same people.

As one of the few ailments of pre-contact Native Americans, earache was treated with herbal remedies. The Mohegans of Connecticut used sumac as a poultice for earaches and ear drops of sumac tea into the affected ear. The Meskwaki of the Midwest used wild ginger in the same manner.

Cherokee belief is that if dreams are told before breakfast they will come true. But think, if one had a good dream, then one is sure to tell it before breakfast.

Legendary figure Will West Long (1870–1947) was an authority on Eastern Band of Cherokee Indians tribal dance, drama, and tradition. He was also an accomplished mask maker. His vast knowledge of Cherokee medicine, carving, music, and dance was recorded to preserve tribal tradition.

The Carlisle Indians football team (from Carlisle Indian Industrial School in Carlisle, Pennsylvania) was composed of Native American students from across the U.S. The team's winning record in intercollegiate competition made it the most successful college football program in history. It was discontinued in 1917, because according to some sources it was too successful at beating non-Indian teams. The Carlisle playbook gave innovations to the game now commonplace in U.S. football.

Wyoming is derived from two Lenni-Lenape/Delaware words *Meche Weamiing* meaning "At the Big Flats." It is also translates as "Large Plains." What is unusual is that the Lenni-Lenape lived almost two thousand miles from the state of Wyoming. They lived originally on the Atlantic Coast, never residing even near the state.

Gary Farmer is a Cayuga Indian actor from Ohsweken, Ontario, on the Six Nations of the Grand River First Nation Reserve in Canada. He has played in numerous well-known movies, including the iconic productions *Powwow Highway* and *Smoke Signals*. Farmer also has a blues band, Gary Farmer and the Troublemakers.

California has the largest number of Indian reservations of any state. There are over a hundred reservations in the state.

The Navajo Reservation is the largest in the U.S. with four-teen to fifteen million acres in Arizona, New Mexico, and Utah. The smallest reservation is the Sheep Ranch Rancheria near Sacramento, California, which is less than one acre, serving the California Valley Miwok tribe.

Nearly one-fourth of all Native American reservation lands, or about thirteen million acres, have some kind of forest cover. In modern times, nearly sixty tribal nations collect from twenty-five percent to one hundred percent of the non-federal monies from timber operations. About 130 tribes belong to what is entitled the "Tribal Timber Consortium."

The name *pecan* derives from the Algonquin Indian word for "nut requiring a stone to crack."

The Native American Music Awards (NAMAS) recognizes great musical achievement by Native American artists. While recognizing an encouraging traditional American Indian music, the NAMAS encompass modern Indian music such as pop, blues, rock, hip-hop, and country. Music by non-Native artists is recognized and honored under the category "Native Heart."

Jim Thorpe of the Sac and Fox Nation, from Prague, Oklahoma, is considered one of the greatest athletes of all time. He won Olympic gold medals in 1912 for the pentathlon and decathlon and played baseball, basketball, and football. Thorpe was voted the Greatest Athlete of the twentieth century in a poll conducted by ABC Sports. He was a graduate of Carlisle Indian Industrial School in Pennsylvania.

Among Native American filmmakers, Chris Eyre, Cheyenne/Arapaho, stands out prominently. Born in Portland, Oregon, the film director and producer's debut film *Smoke Signals* in 1998 won the Sundance Film Festival Filmmakers Trophy and Audience Award. Eyre mostly focuses on films depicting contemporary American Indian life. In 2012 he was appointed film department chair at the Santa Fe University of Art and Design.

The Great Serpent Mound in Adams County, Ohio, is an ancient effigy mound over one thousand feet long. It is designated a National Historic Landmark by the U.S. Department of the Interior. Lenape and Iroquois lore maintain the Allegewi people built the mound in the third century BC. The Serpent Mound is the largest serpent effigy construction in the world.

Well known throughout the United States, Native American celebrity Buffy Sainte-Marie is a Cree Indian singer, songwriter, composer, educator, and political activist. She also appeared regularly on *Sesame Street* from 1976 to 1981. Many awards and honors have been won by her for music, educational work, and activism.

Although in most tribes women did not become warriors, this was not the case among Cherokees. There were Cherokee women who as warriors could follow their husbands and brothers into battle. These were called the War Women or Pretty Women, and were honored in the Nation.

In the very first Tonto and Lone Ranger film, *Hi-Yo Silver* in 1940, Tonto was played by Victor Daniels, a full-blood Cherokee from Muskogee, Oklahoma.

Native American Homes

Adobe houses, multi-unit structures of hard-baked bricks of clay and straw, were built by the Pueblo Indians of the Southwest.

Brush shelters (also called wickiups, lean-tos, *gowa*, etc.) are temporary dwellings usually made for one person. Brush shelters are small, like a camping tent.

Chickees had thick posts supporting a thatched roof and a flat wooden platform raised several feet off the ground. These huts were built by the Seminole Indians in Florida.

Earthen houses refers to several types of semi-subterranean dwellings including Navajo hogans, Sioux earth lodges, subarctic sod houses, and pit houses.

Grass Houses were used in the Southern Plains by the Caddos. They resemble large wigwams but are made with different materials with a wooden frame in a beehive shape.

Longhouses were used by the Iroquois tribes and some of their Algonquian neighbors. They are built similarly to wigwams, with pole frames and elm bark covering. Longhouses are much larger and can hold up to sixty people.

Plank Houses used in the Northwest Coast are made of long, flat planks of cedar wood lashed to a wooden frame.

Tepees are cone-shaped wooden frames with buffalo-hide covering used by Plains tribes. They are carefully designed to set up and break down quickly.

Wattle and daub houses are made by weaving rivercane, wood, and vines into a frame, then coating the frame with plaster. The roof was either thatched with grass or shingled with bark.

Wigwams, also known as birchbark houses, were used by Algonquian Indians. These small houses were made of wooden frames covered with woven mats and sheets of birch bark.

The National Museum of the American Indian opened on the National Mall in Washington, D.C., on September 21, 2004. It is part of the Smithsonian Institution and is devoted to the history, arts, languages, literature, and way of life of the Native peoples of the Western Hemisphere.

The most widespread indigenous religion in the United States is the Native American Church. It originated in Oklahoma and flourishes mostly among the Plains nations. Known also as "the Peyote Road" its principles are American Indian brotherly love, avoidance of alcohol and recreational drug use, and loyalty to family.

A favorite dish of Cherokee families at home and at pow wows is bean bread. Made from cornmeal and pinto beans, it is a culinary delight going back to the Dawn of Time.

The Native American actor Eddie Little Sky was as Oglala Sioux tribal member. He played in thirty-six feature films and in over sixty television shows. Little Sky broke ground as one of the first Native actors to play Indian roles, mostly in westerns.

The Sequoyah Birthplace Museum in East Tennessee opened in 1986. It is dedicated to Sequoyah and to the Cherokees who lived in the area. The museum is owned and operated by the Eastern Band of Cherokee Indians. Exhibits tell the story of Sequoyah and the history of the Cherokee Nation.

A terrapin is a small turtle native to the Southeast. The name *terrapin* is from an Algonquian Indian word. In many parts of the South it is pronounced "tappan."

Tommy Wildcat, a Cherokee keeper of culture, is a flutist, historical storyteller, traditionalist, and lecturer. Wildcat is a founding member of the Cherokee Honor Society. He works with local Oklahoma Cherokee communities and has appeared at pow wows throughout the Southeast. He is from Tahlequah, Oklahoma.

Many tribes in the Southeast, including Cherokees, harvested fish by "poisoning," sinking walnut hulls in a slow-moving fishing hole. The fish are stunned and float to the surface and—*voilà*—fresh fish for dinner.

The thirty-first Vice President of the United States was Charles Curtis, part Native American of Osage, Kaw, and Potawatomi descent. He was raised in the Kaw reservation and was a member of that tribe.

The Southeastern United States had the greatest Native linguistic diversity at the time of European contact of any region in the country. The Iroquoian, Siouan, Algonquin, and Muskhogean languages were all spoken in the region. Interestingly, the Muskhogean languages were only spoken in the South.

Native Americans, like anyone else, sometimes get into the movies just by being "discovered." Will Sampson, for example, was walking to a car dealership in Okmulgee, Oklahoma, to buy a vehicle. A movie producer was stuck by his profile and asked him to consider working in a movie. Sampson said he would be in the movie if the producer would buy him a car. The rest is history.

Three states with the largest Native American populations in the U.S. are California first with 913,382, Arizona second with 294,137, and Oklahoma third with 297,559.

How many children growing up in the woodlands have placed a blade of grass between their thumbs and blown in it to make a high shrill sound? I, for one, did! Did they know Native hunters did so to imitate the cry of fawn in distress, to attract a doe?

Although steaming clams in a pit dug on the beach is considered a New England tradition, few know that this was a Native invention of the Wampanoag people, the tribe that met the pilgrims. Until Natives taught the settlers how to prepare clams in this manner, the colonists thought the tasty seafood was poisonous.

According to U.S. studies, Native Americans had medicinal uses for 2,564 species of plants. So far, over two hundred plants that were used for Indian medicine are now part of the U.S. pharmacopoeia. Cherokee medicine men and women had, on average, memorized eight hundred plants to treat their patients.

In the early nineteenth century, non-Indian herbal doctors began using Indian botanical medicines. This enthusiasm for Native cures resulted in the creation of patent medicines.

The first American Indian newspaper was the *Cherokee Phoenix,* first published by the Cherokee Nation in 1828. The paper was printed with columns in Cherokee and English. Today publications in Cherokee range from legal documents to comic books.

The game of basketball, so popular today, was begun by Native Americans three thousand years ago. The game was played by Olmec Indians in what is now southern Mexico with balls made from rubber. Basketball is now popular on reservations throughout the U.S.

Hot springs were used by Native peoples whenever available. A good example are the springs in Hot Springs National Park in Arkansas. These hot springs were considered neutral ground where even nations at war could meet in peace.

The Iroquoian and Muskhogean languages, while completely different, have the same basic word for buffalo: *Yansa*. Often wondered who borrowed the word from whom. Muscogees from Cherokees, or vice versa?

Among the many methods used by Native Americans to catch fish, the trotline was very popular. A trotline was a length of fishing line to which baited hooks were attached, stretched across a waterway or a small lake. The trotline was adopted by the colonists and is still used to this day in the South..

Chronic indigestion was treated by many Southeastern peoples with tea made of wintergreen root. In the north, the Wyandot and other Nations treated the ailment with juice extracted from cedar tree branches.

On and near the southeastern Atlantic coast there were more than twenty-five small Siouan-speaking tribes. Siouan is also the language of the mighty Lakota (Sioux) of the Northern Plains. Could the Southeast have been the original home of the Sioux?

The phrase "Native American Renaissance" refers to the great increase in literary works by American Indian authors in the latter twentieth century. This Renaissance followed the publication of the Pulitzer Prize-winning *House Made of Dawn* by N. Scott Momaday in 1969.

The name *Texas* comes from the word *Teysha* in the Caddo language, meaning "Hello, Friend." The Spaniards applied the name to any friendly tribe. They called the Caddo confederacy in West Texas "The Kingdom of the Tejas" or "Allies."

Among all the nations of the Southeast, meat was always well-cooked, never eaten rare. The one exception was the case of the noted Cherokee warrior Bloody Fellow. He got his name not from fighting his enemies, but because he liked his meat rare, not well done. This seemed so strange that he was called Bloody Fellow.

The name of the state of Oregon is derived from *Oyer-un-Gun*, a Shoshone word meaning "Place of Plenty." Other sources maintain it is a Lakota word meaning "Great River to the West."

Inuit (Eskimo) in Alaska used portable space heaters made of moss soaked in animal fat set on a walrus tusk that held whale blubber. These heaters made homes very warm and comfortable even in below-zero outdoor temperatures.

Grits originated with Southeastern Indians as a form of instant breakfast food. Grits are simply ground corn meal, that when poured into boiling water becomes a breakfast staple, thanks to Native American culinary skills.

In the Midwest, Nations such as the Mesquakie, Ojibwa, and Potawatomi used various plants to ease labor pains during pregnancy. One plant, blue cohosh, was made into a tea and was so effective that colonists later used it for "female troubles."

Wherever corn was grown in the U.S., Indian people also prepared it as hominy. It was made by soaking corn in wood ash water or lime water. Hominy remains a popular dish to this day in the South.

Native Americans in the North and Southeast used natural repellants to remain insect-free. The Iroquois mixed chestnut oil with bear grease to repel summertime bugs. In the Southeast, Indian peoples used pounded goldenseal root mixed with bear fat for the same results.

Native Americans had a number of plant remedies for headaches. The Zuni of New Mexico made a tea from corn smut for relief. Cherokees sometimes used a headband filled with peach tree leaves for headache pain.

Many tribal parents in the Southern and Western Woodlands made corn-husk dolls for their children. But among the Iroquois, parents took care not to make a face on the doll, as they believed dolls with faces could come alive and would do evil to human beings.

The dreamcatchers that are now mass-produced began with the Ojibwe people in the Midwest. They were a protective charm for babies, to make sure they had pleasant dreams.

These handmade objects are often based on a willow hoop, on which is woven a loose net or web. The dreamcatcher is then decorated with sacred items such as feathers and beads.

Interestingly enough, many Native people wore socks. In the colder climates, Indians wore socks inside moccasins or boots for warmth. Socks were made from various materials, including the skins of rabbits, badgers, caribou, muskrats, and moose. Other Indians in warmer areas wove socks from plants such as yucca and types of grass.

Calendars were developed by Native peoples in North, Central, and South America. American Indian calendars were so exact that some were off by only nineteen minutes.

Tobogganing and snowshoeing are popular winter sports first developed by early Natives. *Toboggan* is derived from the Algonquian *odabaggan,* a sled designed to help hunting parties drag their game over the snow.

Native Americans make their livelihoods in various ways, as do others in today's world. There are American Indian ranchers, physicians, factory workers, carpenters, construction workers, lawyers, cooks, rodeo cowboys, farmers, secretaries, radio announcers, dentists, accountants, astronauts, soldiers, engineers, legislators, salespersons, actors, musicians, veterinarians, foresters, janitors, authors, truckers, police officers, educators, scientists, psychologists, and commercial fishermen. There are also park rangers, craft workers, artists, and tribal administrators. The list goes on and on and on.

Recommended Pow Wows

Pow wows are the way in which Native Americans come together to dance and sing, renew old friendships, and make new ones. Pow wows are also a time for others to experience Native American culture firsthand—and to enjoy the songs and dances, learn the customs, taste traditional foods, and see magnificent Native American dress.

No one knows for sure how they started. Many believe the celebrations evolved from the war dance of the Societies of the Ponca, while others from the Southern Plains tribes. Either way, the songs and dances preserve a rich heritage of religious, social and even war traditions. Singers are highly regarded and respected members of the community.

Some of the larger pow wows are:

Denver Pow Wow Denver Coliseum – Denver, Colorado www.denvermarchpowwow.org	March
Gathering of Nations Albuquerque, New Mexico www.gatheringofnations.com	April
Red Earth Festival Oklahoma City, Oklahoma www.redearth.org	June
Grand Celebration Powwow Hinckley, Minnesota www.millelacsojibwe.org	June
Midnight Sun Intertribal Powwow Fairbanks, Alaska www.midnightsunpowwow.com	July

United Tribes International Powwow   September
Bismarck, North Dakota
www.unitedtribespowwow.com

Morongo Thunder and Lightning Pow Wow   September
Cabazon, California
www.morongocasinoresort.com/wp-contentpowwow/pow2.php

Tennessee State Pow-Wow   October
Nashville, Tennessee
www.naiatn.org/powwow/index.html

Moundville Native American Festival   October
Moundville, Alabama
www.alabama.travel/upcoming-events/moundville-native-american-
festival-2014

Pahrump Powwowa   November
Pahrump, Nevada
www.powwows.com

Museums

National Museum of the American Indian
Fourth Street and Independence Avenue, SW
Washington, D.C. 20560
202-633-5285

Big Bear Native American Museum
Chisholm Trail Museum
2929 West Henderson Street
Cleburne, TX 76033
817-648-0989

C.H. Nash Museum at Chucalissa
1987 Indian Village Dr.
Memphis, TN 38109

Eiteljorg Museum of American Indians and Western Art
500 West Washington St.
Indianapolis, IN 46204
317-636-9378

Five Civilized Tribes Museum
1101 Honor Heights Drive
Muskogee, OK 74401
918-683-1701

Heard Museum of American Indian Art & History
2301 North Central Avenue
Phoenix, AZ 85004
602-252-8840

Indian Museum of North America
Crazy Horse Memorial
12151 Avenue of Chiefs
Crazy Horse, SD 57730
605-673-4681

Mashantucket Pequot Museum & Research Center
110 Pequot Trail
Mashantucket, CT 06338
800-411-9671

Mitchell Museum of the American Indian
3001 Central Street
Evanston, IL 60201
847-475-1030

Museum of the Cherokee Indian
589 Tsali Boulevard
Cherokee, NC 28719
828-497-3481

Wheelwright Museum of the American Indian
704 Camino Lejo
Santa Fe, NM 87505
800-607-4636

When you arise in the morning,
give thanks for the morning light,
for your life and strength.
Give thanks for your food
and the joy of living.
If you see no reason for
giving thanks, the fault
lies within yourself.

Tecumseh
Shawnee Chief